YOU ARE BRAVE

May these pages inspire you to open your heart.
In vulnerability, we find strength, resilience,
and the power to heal.

YOUR VOICE MATTERS

Are you enjoying this book? Consider sharing your experience with us on Amazon. Your review not only helps our book reach more readers but also inspires fellow seekers on their journeys of growth and self-discovery. Don't forget that Amazon allows you to post photos, so you can share your artwork as well.

YOUR REVIEW MAKES A DIFFERENCE
tinyurl.com/truebookreview

Your Fellow Artist & Sojourner

Julie True

DEDICATION

To My Dear Friend Brenda.
You have always shown up, been vulnerable, and reflected strength and resilience that is beyond comprehension. You have so much grace. I am so glad that I have had the opportunity to know you.

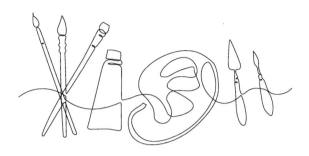

Your Canvas for Self-Expression

Dive into experimentation on the practice pages, where there's no judgment—only freedom of expression. Here, you can play with colors, blend shades, and explore various techniques without fear of imperfection. It's a canvas where creativity flows freely, just waiting for your artistic potential to flourish.

CHOOSING YOUR TOOLS
Colored Pencils or Markers

While I recommend <u>colored pencils</u> for their precision and control, I wholeheartedly encourage you to embrace your preferences. If markers are your chosen medium, go ahead! Simply slip an additional sheet of paper behind the page to safeguard the designs beneath.

YOUR JOURNEY, YOUR CHOICES.

I would love to see your favorite completed picture send it to gallery@truehuesart.com. When you do we will send you a free coloring page from the next book! Share your work on social and use the hashtag #truehuesart so we can see it too!

UNLEASHING YOUR INNER STRENGTH AND WISDOM

Resilience and self-awareness are your pillars of strength, enabling you to rebound from setbacks, embrace change, and emerge even stronger. They are your guides to emotional balance, personal growth, and values-driven decision-making.

Within these pages, you'll find intricate designs that invite you to unleash your creativity and reflect upon the radiant spirit within you. Each stroke of color is a declaration of your boundless potential, and every journal entry is a testament to your unique story.

TRUE SELF-WORTH IS NOT FOUND IN THE REFLECTION OF THE
MIRROR OR THE NUMBERS ON THE SCALE;
IT'S IN THE IMMEASURABLE KINDNESS AND BOUNDLESS LOVE
YOU SHARE WITH THE WORLD.

You don't need their approval;
you are enough.

Journaling

Recall a moment of inner strength in the face of adversity.
Describe how you felt and what empowered you.

_____

_____

_____

_____

_____

_____

_____

_____

_____

_____

_____

Born in 1945, Les Brown's life began with adversity. Abandoned at birth and labeled "educable mentally retarded" as a child, he grew up feeling the weight of rejection and the harsh limitations society placed on him. Poverty, a lack of formal education, and the constant barrage of people telling him he would never succeed became his daily reality. But instead of succumbing to these obstacles, Les transformed his pain into power. With relentless determination and a deep belief in his potential, he shattered every barrier in his path. Today, as a world-renowned motivational speaker and author, Les inspires millions with his story of resilience, reminding us that no matter where you start or how insurmountable the odds seem, you can rise above. His journey is a testament to the power of self-belief and the truth that we all have greatness within us—waiting to be unleashed.

You are the only real obstacle in your path to a fulfilling life.

LES BROWN

Don't let the bad days make you think
you have a bad life.

Journal Prompts for Reflecting on Your Personal Values:

What core values do you live by, and why are they important to you? Reflect on the principles that guide your life, like honesty, compassion, or perseverance. How have these values shaped your decisions and interactions?

_____
_____
_____
_____
_____
_____
_____
_____
_____
_____
_____
_____

BRENDON BURCHARD

Brendon faced a near-fatal car accident at 19, which left him grappling with life-threatening injuries. This life-altering incident ignited his passion for personal development and self-improvement. Rising from the depths of despair, he dedicated himself to mastering the art of motivation, leadership, and high performance. Overcoming his physical and emotional scars, Burchard has become a highly sought-after motivational speaker, author, and life coach, touching the lives of millions with his teachings on achieving one's highest potential.

IN THE MIDST OF CHALLENGES,
OUR VALUES ARE OUR GUIDING STARS,
LEADING US TOWARD A BRIGHTER FUTURE.
Brendon Burchard

PRACTICE MINDFUL DECISION-MAKING

- Slow down your decision process and be intentional about considering values:
- Take time to pause and reflect before deciding
- Visualize how each option would look if fully aligned with your values
- Notice any inner tension between choices and your principles

MINDFULNESS HELPS YOU TUNE INTO VALUE CONSIDERATIONS YOU MIGHT OTHERWISE OVERLOOK.

Journaling

THINK ABOUT THE VALUES, BELIEFS, STRENGTHS, AND CHARACTERISTICS THAT MAKE YOU UNIQUELY "YOU." Consider how these qualities have contributed to your inner strength, resilience, and overall well-being. Reflect on specific instances where your authentic self has shone through, empowering you to overcome challenges and obstacles. As you explore these aspects of your identity, recognize the importance of embracing and nurturing your authentic self, as it can be a source of tremendous inner strength and a compass for personal growth.

_____
_____
_____
_____
_____
_____
_____
_____
_____
_____

SIMON SINEK

Simon Sinek is a renowned author and speaker, best known for his insightful concept of the "Golden Circle." This principle is centered on a fundamental idea: the significance of "Why" in understanding purpose and motivation. The "Golden Circle" represents three concentric circles, with "Why" at the core, followed by "How," and "What." Sinek's concept stresses that truly impactful individuals and organizations start with a clear understanding of their core beliefs and purpose (the "Why"), which then informs the strategies (the "How") and tangible actions (the "What"). This principle is vital for self-discovery, as it encourages individuals to explore their inner motivations and values, providing a profound framework to unearth their true purpose and drive.

Values are the compass that helps us navigate through the stormy seas of life, always pointing us in the right direction.

Simon Sinek

VALUES ARE THE COMPASS GUIDING US THROUGH LIFE'S STORMS, ALWAYS POINTING US IN THE RIGHT DIRECTION.

Journaling

What ethical, personal, or spiritual beliefs resonate with you and guide your life? EXPLORE THE WHY. Your core principles and their profound influence on your internal dialogue and motivations. Think about why these values are essential to you – for instance, if kindness is a core value, consider how it shapes your motivations to make a positive impact on others and the positive self-talk it generates, ultimately revealing the profound significance of these guiding lights in your life.

_____

_____

_____

_____

_____

_____

_____

_____

_____

_____

_____

ZIG ZIGLAR

Zig Ziglar (1926-2012) was an iconic American author, motivational speaker, and salesman renowned for his inspirational messages and life-changing wisdom. Growing up during the Great Depression, Ziglar's journey from humble beginnings to becoming a prominent figure in personal development is truly inspiring. His speeches and writings resonated with millions, emphasizing the power of a positive attitude, goal setting, and hard work. Through his extensive career, Ziglar encouraged countless individuals to unlock their full potential and reach their aspirations, leaving a lasting legacy in the world of personal growth and motivation.

YOU DON'T HAVE TO BE GREAT TO START, BUT YOU HAVE TO START TO BE GREAT.

– Zig Ziglar

BREAK DOWN LARGER AMBITIONS INTO MANAGEABLE TASKS. START WITH SIMPLE, ACHIEVABLE GOALS THAT CAN LEAD YOU TOWARD GREATER ACCOMPLISHMENTS.

Journaling

DIG DEEP - EXPLORE ONE FINAL VALUE.

As the final of four prompts for values, take a moment to explore the essence of your true self. Reflect on the values or principles that steadfastly guide your life, such as integrity, empathy, or determination. Consider how these values have been your unwavering support during trying times, like how integrity led you to make an honest yet difficult decision or how empathy provided solace to someone in need. Delve deeper into the core principles that illuminate your path and examine how these specific values have played a pivotal role in shaping your character during challenging moments.

ECKHART TOLLE'

Eckhart Tolle experienced significant personal and emotional turmoil, including depression and a profound sense of emptiness. This inner turmoil had reached a breaking point, leading to a pivotal moment in his life when he contemplated suicide. It was during this moment of extreme despair that he experienced a profound spiritual awakening, which marked the turning point in his life and eventually led to his work as a spiritual teacher and author. His journey from despair to enlightenment is a central theme in his teachings and writings.

**IN CHALLENGING TIMES, YOUR VALUES ARE THE ANCHOR THAT KEEPS YOU STEADY WHEN EVERYTHING ELSE IS SHIFTING.
ECKHART TOLLE**

GET A PREVIEW OF THE NEXT BOOK & FREE COLORING PAGES
TRULYREFLECTING.COM

Are you enjoying this book? Consider sharing your experience with us on Amazon.
Don't forget Amazon allows you to post photos,
so you can share your artwork as well!
OPEN YOUR CAMERA APP AND SCAN THE CODE
you will be linked directly to my author page and all my the books on Amazon.

Journaling

Share the details of a recent setback or challenge you've faced, no matter how big or small. Explore how you can reframe this experience to see it as an opportunity for personal growth. Consider the lessons learned, the strengths revealed, and the potential positive outcomes that can emerge from this adversity.

By re-evaluating setbacks through a growth-oriented lens, you can harness their transformative power and use them as stepping stones on your journey toward self-improvement and resilience.

BRENÉ BROWN

Her transformative path began with personal struggles as she confronted feelings of vulnerability, shame, and self-doubt. Her determination to understand and overcome these challenges led her to years of research on human emotions and connection.

Through her groundbreaking work, Brown has since become a renowned author, speaker, and vulnerability expert, empowering people worldwide to embrace their authenticity, cultivate resilience, and build deeper connections. Her own triumph over adversity stands as a beacon of hope for those striving to navigate the complexities of the human experience with courage and grace.

Adversity introduces a person to themselves. Embrace your challenges; they hold the key to your growth.

BRENE BROWN

ADVERSITY WHISPERS TRUTHS
ABOUT YOUR RESILIENCE AND
POWER. LEAN IN AND LISTEN;
IT'S A REMINDER OF THE DEPTH
OF YOUR STRENGTH.

Journaling

LIST THREE <u>FEARS</u> THAT HAVE IMPACTED YOUR LIFE.
WHAT SMALL STEPS CAN YOU TAKE TO CONFRONT THESE FEARS?

Begin by bravely listing your fears and understanding how they've impacted your thoughts, emotions, and actions. Then, create a roadmap for conquering each fear with practical steps like gaining knowledge, seeking support, setting achievable goals, practicing mindfulness, challenging negative beliefs, and gradual exposure. Conquer the unknown by taking the first step, which could involve gathering information and answering the "WHY?" you have this fear.

Embrace this courageous, step-by-step journey to face your fears, seek assistance, and celebrate your progress as you go.

_____
_____
_____
_____
_____
_____
_____
_____
_____
_____

BETHANY HAMILTON

Bethany Hamilton, born in 1990, is an inspirational figure known for her remarkable journey from tragedy to triumph. At the age of 13, she suffered a life-altering shark attack that resulted in the loss of her left arm. Despite this devastating setback, Bethany's unyielding determination, unwavering spirit, and her love for surfing propelled her forward. With sheer resilience and unshakable dedication, she not only returned to the waves but went on to become a professional surfer, inspiring countless individuals worldwide with her story of courage and triumph over adversity.

COURAGE DOESN'T MEAN YOU DON'T GET AFRAID. COURAGE MEANS YOU DON'T LET FEAR STOP YOU.

Bethany Hamilton

FEAR MAY VISIT, BUT IT'S YOUR COURAGE THAT STAYS. TRUST IT— IT'S WHAT CARRIES YOU THROUGH.

Journaling

WRITE ABOUT A DREAM YOU'VE HELD ONTO, EVEN DURING CHALLENGING MOMENTS. WHAT GIVES YOU HOPE?

Share the essence of this dream, why it's meaningful to you, and how it has served as a beacon of hope during trying times. Explore the specific elements of this dream that continue to inspire and motivate you, as well as the source of your hope in achieving it. By delving into this dream and the hope it provides, you can gain a deeper understanding of your aspirations and what fuels your determination in the face of life's challenges.

_____
_____
_____
_____
_____
_____
_____
_____
_____
_____

SUZANNE COLLINS

Growing up in a military family, her father's Vietnam War deployment forged themes of conflict and sacrifice early in her life. Suzanne Collins found solace in books during his absence, sparking her passion for storytelling. Her career in children's television writing refined her narrative skills, but it was a conversation with her father that inspired her iconic "Hunger Games" trilogy, addressing society's desensitization to violence. This series propelled her to global fame, showcasing Suzanne Collins as a master storyteller who conquered personal and societal challenges through her gripping narratives.

HOPE IS THE ONLY THING STRONGER THAN FEAR.
- SUZANNE COLLINS

INNER PEACE IS A QUIET STRENGTH—
A REMINDER THAT, NO MATTER THE
CHAOS AROUND YOU, YOU HAVE THE
POWER TO RETURN TO YOURSELF.

Journaling

IMAGINE YOUR IDEAL FUTURE.

Envision your dream future in intricate detail, encompassing your aspirations and objectives. Then, transition to the present moment and contemplate the tangible actions you can undertake today to bring that vision nearer. Consider setting goals, acquiring new skills, nurturing relationships, or modifying your lifestyle. This prompt bridges the gap between your long-term aspirations and immediate actions, empowering you to proactively shape your desired future.

_____
_____
_____
_____
_____
_____
_____
_____
_____
_____
_____
_____
_____

C.S. LEWIS

Born in 1898 in Belfast, Ireland, C.S. Lewis experienced early loss and the devastation of his mother's death. World War I further shaped his worldview, exposing him to the horrors of conflict. Amid these trials, Lewis turned to writing for solace. His exploration of faith, notably in the "Chronicles of Narnia," allowed him to triumph over personal turmoil, inspiring millions with his profound insights and masterful storytelling. Lewis's journey from grief and wartime experiences to becoming one of the most influential Christian writers of the 20th century is a testament to the resilience of the human spirit and the power of God to transcend tragedy.

"You are never too old to set another goal or to dream a new dream.
C.S. Lewis

When you know your worth, no storm can pull you off course.

Journaling

Recall a moment of pure joy or happiness. What made it special, and how can you create more of these moments? Revisit a moment of sheer happiness and analyze its ingredients for a more joyful life. Dive into the details, the people, and the circumstances that made it extraordinary. Then, chart a course for intentionally creating more such moments. Explore choices, habits, and mindset shifts that can usher in joy. By rekindling these cherished memories and implementing strategies for more, you infuse your life with an abundance of positivity and fulfillment.

_____

_____

_____

_____

_____

_____

_____

_____

_____

_____

_____

RALPH MARSTON

Ralph Marston confronted personal challenges and setbacks that could have easily crushed his spirit. However, his unshakable faith in the power of positive thinking defined his journey. Despite physical limitations and hardships, Marston dedicated himself to inspiring others through his writings. Renowned for his motivational quotes and "The Daily Motivator" newsletter, he empowered countless individuals to embrace positivity and determination in the face of life's trials.

**HAPPINESS IS A CHOICE, NOT A RESULT. NOTHING WILL MAKE YOU HAPPY UNTIL YOU CHOOSE TO BE HAPPY.
RALPH MARSTON**

The power to be happy lives in you;
it's a choice, a light you carry, no
matter what surrounds you.

EMPOWERING YOUR CONFIDENCE AND SELF-WORTH

Nurture self-esteem and self-confidence to reveal a positive self-image, enhanced resilience, and deeper self-acceptance. These guided journal prompts will empower your journey towards a stronger, more confident you.

CHRISTIAN D. LARSON

Written in 1907, "The Great Within" by Christian D. Larson is a self-help and personal development book that explores the human mind's power and potential for transformation. Larson delves into the concept of the inner self, highlighting how our thoughts and beliefs shape our lives. The book stresses the significance of positive thinking, self-belief, and self-worth in attaining personal goals and happiness. It provides practical advice on unlocking one's inner potential for a more fulfilling and successful life. Larson's enduring work continues to inspire readers to harness their inner selves for personal growth and well-being.

Believe in yourself and all that you are.
Know that there is something inside you
that is greater than any obstacle.

CHRISTIAN D. LARSON

Happiness blooms within, nurtured by the choice to see beauty in every moment—even the quiet, imperfect ones.

Journaling

"THE POWER OF YOUR SELF-TALK"

Your self-talk is a mighty force. The words we whisper to ourselves, the stories we create in our minds, mold our perceptions, beliefs, and, ultimately, our reality. It's the beginning of our journey: discovering the messages we continually tell ourselves. This initial step is crucial in breaking free from self-doubt and despair, replacing them with the comforting embrace of self-compassion and confidence. Take a moment to identify a self-defeating phrase you frequently use. WRITE IT DOWN. Now, when you catch yourself saying it, consciously substitute it with words of kindness and affirmation. (BE SURE WRITE DOWN THE POSITIVE PHRASE) This simple act of self-compassion can profoundly transform your self-relationship.

This simple act of self-compassion can be a profound shift in the way you relate to yourself.

_____

_____

_____

_____

_____

_____

_____

_____

_____

_____

JORDAN BELFORT

Born in 1962, he initially achieved success on Wall Street but spiraled into a world of financial corruption and deceit, leading to his arrest and imprisonment for securities fraud and money laundering. After serving his sentence, Belfort transformed his life. He channeled his experiences into becoming an author and motivational speaker, using his insights to guide others toward ethical success. His transition from a life of crime to one of redemption and self-improvement exemplifies the potency of personal growth and resilience in overcoming adversity.

The only thing standing between you and your goal is the story you keep telling yourself about why you can't achieve it.

Jordan Belfort

YOUR POTENTIAL IS WAITING BEYOND THE DOUBTS YOU'VE OUTGROWN. STEP INTO A NEW STORY THAT BELIEVES IN YOUR SUCCESS.

Journaling

Harness your inner strength and creativity by envisioning your inner cheerleader, a supportive force that counteracts your inner critic. Picture this champion as your personal wellspring of motivation and encouragement. Write yourself an encouraging letter as if you are writing to encourage a friend.

_____
_____
_____
_____
_____
_____
_____
_____
_____
_____
_____

ELIZABETH GILBERT

Gilbert, after enduring early-life challenges, navigated a turbulent divorce that prompted deep soul-searching. Her life-altering journey, chronicled in "Eat, Pray, Love," took her to Italy, India, and Indonesia, in pursuit of healing, self-discovery, and the true essence of life. This transformative odyssey resonated with readers globally, encouraging them to seek their own paths to happiness and fulfillment. Elizabeth Gilbert's narrative, from despair to triumph, illustrates the resilience of the human spirit and the enriching potential of self-discovery.

EMBRACE THE GLORIOUS MESS THAT YOU ARE.
ELIZABETH GILBERT

YOU ARE BEAUTIFULLY IMPERFECT,
A MASTERPIECE IN PROGRESS.
EMBRACE EVERY COLOR AND
STROKE THAT MAKES YOU, YOU.

Journaling

Recall a moment when you displayed courage in the face of fear, reflecting on the challenges you conquered. Analyze the fears that were present and the strategies you used to triumph over them. This introspection reveals your reservoir of resilience, strength, and the courage to confront adversity. Use this reflection as a wellspring of inspiration for future challenges and a reminder of your inner reserves to overcome them.

_____

_____

_____

_____

_____

_____

_____

_____

_____

_____

_____

Rabindranath Tagore

He was the first non-European Nobel Prize in Literature laureate, left an indelible mark through his unparalleled literary contributions. He played a crucial role in fostering cross-cultural appreciation between the East and the West, becoming a symbol of India's cultural richness. Amid his soaring achievements, Tagore faced profound personal losses, enduring the untimely death of his mother, wife, and children. These heart-wrenching tragedies significantly impacted his emotional well-being. Nonetheless, his enduring legacy thrives through his poetry, music, and philosophical writings, continuing to inspire and uplift people worldwide.

YOU HOLD THE POWER TO MOVE
BEYOND FEAR. TAKE THE PLUNGE;
ONLY THROUGH ACTION CAN YOU
REACH NEW SHORES.

Journaling

WHAT ARE SOME WAYS TO TAKE CARE OF YOURSELF AND SHOW SELF-LOVE? LIST SPECIFIC ACTIONS.

Nurture self-love and self-care through tangible steps: prioritize meditation, rest, exercise, hobbies, balanced nutrition, setting boundaries, and seeking support. Embrace positive self-talk and self-compassion, recognizing that self-care is a vital contributor to your well-being and happiness.

"USE YOUR KIND WORDS"

As a mother, I've stumbled upon a guiding principle that has been a lifeline in navigating the turbulent sea of self-talk. I've realized that if I wouldn't utter certain words to a child, then why on earth would I say them to myself? Why do we often extend kindness, patience, and encouraging words to those we love while being so harsh and unforgiving about ourselves? One of the kindest things we can do FOR ourselves is to speak kindly TO ourselves.

THE WORDS YOU SPEAK TO YOURSELF
SHAPE YOUR HEART. CHOOSE ONES
THAT LIFT YOU UP AND REMIND YOU
OF YOUR WORTH.

Journaling

**IDENTIFY 3 ACTIVITIES THAT DEEPLY RESONATE WITH YOU,
THE ONES THAT MAKE YOU FEEL TRULY ALIVE.**

Delve into the experiences and activities that ignite a profound sense of vitality and joy within you, those moments that make you feel truly alive. Whether it's engaging in creative pursuits, spending time in nature, pursuing a particular hobby, or connecting with loved ones, consider what activities bring you that sense of vibrancy and authenticity. Then, consider how to integrate more of these experiences into your daily life for increased well-being and fulfillment.

_____

_____

_____

_____

_____

_____

_____

_____

_____

ALBERT SCHWEITZER

Born in 1875, he was a gifted theologian, musician, and philosopher. However, his true calling emerged when he encountered the impoverished and ill in Africa while working as a medical missionary. Witnessing the dire need for healthcare, Schweitzer abandoned his comfortable life and dedicated himself to serving the people of Gabon as a doctor. His commitment to the alleviation of suffering led to the establishment of a hospital in Lambarene, where he and his wife tirelessly worked for the well-being of the local population. Schweitzer's contributions to medicine and humanitarianism were internationally recognized, and he was awarded the Nobel Peace Prize in 1952. His journey from privilege to a life of humble service reflects the immense impact one individual can have in making the world a better place.

Success is not the key to happiness.
Happiness is the key to success.
If you love what you are doing,
you will be successful.

Albert Schweitzer

Cultivate joy, and you'll discover
the true richness of achievement.

Journaling

Reflect on a time when you felt beautiful both inside and out.

How can you create more moments like this?

This is an invitation to delve into a memory where you were not only physically attractive but also radiated a sense of inner beauty. As you reflect on this moment, consider the circumstances, emotions, and experiences that contributed to this profound feeling.

_____
_____
_____
_____
_____
_____
_____
_____
_____
_____

PRACTICE PAGE
COLOR SWATCHES

John O'Donohue

Irish poet, author, and philosopher who left an indelible mark on the world through his insightful and profoundly spiritual writings. Born in County Clare, Ireland, O'Donohue's work often explored themes of human connection with nature, spirituality, and the profound mysteries of life. He authored several books, including the best-selling "Anam Cara," which touched the hearts of readers worldwide. O'Donohue's eloquent and deeply reflective prose resonated with those seeking a deeper understanding of the human spirit and the interconnectedness of all life. His untimely passing in 2008 marked the end of a life devoted to profound spiritual exploration and the power of words to illuminate the human experience.

"True beauty is a ray that springs
from the sacred depths of the soul."

John O'Donohue

True beauty is found in your essence, a reflection of your heart's kindness and your soul's strength. Let it shine brightly.

TRIUMPHING OVER CHALLENGES AND NURTURING PERSONAL GROWTH

This section is essential as it empowers you to confront and conquer life's obstacles, fostering personal growth and resilience. By addressing challenges head-on and utilizing personal strengths, you can transform setbacks into opportunities for self-improvement.

Every challenge is a chance to grow; embrace your strengths and turn obstacles into stepping stones on your path to greatness.

Journaling

LIST YOUR STRENGTHS AND ACCOMPLISHMENTS.
DESCRIBE HOW THEY'VE HELPED YOU OVERCOME CHALLENGES.

Identify your personal attributes, skills, and achievements of which you're proud. Reflect on how these strengths and successes have aided you in surmounting life's challenges. How have they helped you tackle problems, endure tough times, or face adversity?

_____
_____
_____
_____
_____
_____
_____
_____
_____
_____
_____
_____

This self-reflection empowers you to acknowledge your resilience and the resources you possess for conquering future obstacles, fostering increased self-confidence and empowerment in navigating life's ups and downs.

Haemin Sunim

Haemin Sunim, born in South Korea, is a globally renowned Zen Buddhist monk, author, and teacher known for his wisdom on mindfulness, inner peace, and meaningful living. With training spanning Korea and the United States, he uniquely combines Eastern and Western perspectives in his mindfulness and spiritual teachings. Sunim's life is a testament to his dedication to helping individuals find tranquility and contentment amid modern challenges. Through his influential books, such as "The Things You Can See Only When You Slow Down," he has inspired a worldwide audience to embrace mindfulness and enhance their well-being. Haemin Sunim's work is a guiding light in our fast-paced, interconnected world. Haemin Sunim's work and teachings serve as a beacon of wisdom in our fast-paced, interconnected world.

THROUGH SELF-REFLECTION, WE CAN FIND OUR TRUE SELVES,
CONNECT WITH OUR INNER WISDOM,
AND LEARN TO NAVIGATE THE ROUGH WATERS OF LIFE
WITH CLARITY AND GRACE.
HAEMIN SUNIM

When you turn inward, you connect with your deepest truths. Let that connection be your compass, steering you through life's complexities.

Journaling

Consider a recent emotional challenge where your reaction didn't align with your desired response. How can you react differently and more constructively in similar situations in the future? When confronted with emotions that might not benefit you, "opposite action" is about deliberately opting for a more beneficial response. This technique aids in cultivating emotional regulation and more effective coping strategies, fostering personal growth and resilience. By outlining how you might respond differently in similar situations down the road, you're actively working to improve your emotional well-being and mitigate the influence of challenging emotions. Consider using 'and' statements. "I can be upset by their treatment, AND I can remain calm and in control of my words and actions."

_____

_____

_____

_____

_____

_____

_____

_____

_____

_____

CHARLES R. SWINDOLL

He began his quest in the ordinary world, facing personal hardships and financial challenges. However, he transformed these initial setbacks into a transformative adventure, crossing the threshold into a world of spiritual exploration and wisdom. Along his path, he encountered mentors such as unwavering determination and unshakable faith, acquiring the tools of inspiration and guidance. Swindoll's elixir, his profound messages of hope and resilience, became the boon he shared with countless individuals on their own quests for meaning and spiritual growth. His life's journey reflects the classic hero's path of trials, growth, and eventual triumph, inspiring others to navigate their unique paths to greatness.

**LIFE IS 10% WHAT HAPPENS TO US
AND 90% HOW WE REACT TO IT.
CHARLES R. SWINDOLL**

YOUR POWER LIES IN YOUR RESPONSE.
CHOOSE TO REACT WITH RESILIENCE
AND POSITIVITY, AND WATCH HOW
YOUR PERSPECTIVE TRANSFORMS
YOUR LIFE.

Practical Exercise

Here are some basic skills for addressing emotional overwhelm and emotional distress include immediate responses, such as:

Breathing: Focusing on your breath to regain composure and calm during heightened emotional states.

Tense and Relax: Practicing progressive muscle relaxation techniques to release physical tension associated with emotional distress.

Grounding: Employing grounding exercises to reconnect with the present moment and reduce feelings of dissociation or anxiety.

Change locations, go outside, or splash water on your face.

Find objects in a room that are the same color.

WHEN YOU FIND THOSE RESOURCES THAT RESONATE WITH YOU AND MAKE A LIST.
*Create a sticky note and put it in a location where you can see that you regularly get dysregulated to remind you in the midst of distress.

_____

_____

_____

_____

_____

_____

_____

DEBORAH DAY

Deborah Day, an accomplished author, therapist, and motivational speaker, has dedicated her life to helping individuals discover their inner strength and foster personal growth. With a commitment to empowering others through her writings and presentations, she offers valuable insights on a range of topics, including mental health, relationships, and self-discovery.

Every act of self-care is a seed planted for your growth. Water them with love, and watch yourself flourish in the light of your dreams.

Journaling

IDENTIFYING AND CHALLENGING YOUR FEARS AND SELF-DOUBTS

This prompt might be easier with insight from a loving partner or friend. Sometimes, our negative thoughts can hold us captive, and we can't see contradicting evidence to challenge a deeply held fear or doubt. Who can you ask for support?

- Recognize a specific fear or self-doubt. Just one.
- Could you break down that negative thought? What are you telling yourself?
- List Contradicting Evidence. Be Honest and Draw from experience.

_____

_____

_____

_____

_____

_____

_____

Challenge Your Belief. It isn't always...and it isn't never... there's a middle ground that I can build upon.

DENIS WAITLEY

Denis Waitley, a celebrated author and motivational speaker, has left an indelible mark on the world of personal development and self-improvement. With a profound understanding of the human psyche, Waitley's wisdom has touched countless lives. His quote, "It's not what you are that holds you back; it's what you think you are not," encapsulates his philosophy of overcoming self-doubt and realizing one's full potential. Waitley's accomplishments include a prolific writing career, where he authored best-selling books, and his impactful work as a speaker, inspiring individuals to break free from the constraints of self-limiting beliefs. His life is a testament to the transformative power of self-belief, resilience, and the pursuit of one's true potential.

You are an uncut gemstone of priceless value. Cut and polish your potential with knowledge, skills and service and you will be in great demand throughout your life.

Denis Waitley

Like an uncut gemstone,
your potential is immense.
Embrace learning and
growth to reveal the
brilliance that lies within you.

Journaling

The Power of Reframing: Take one of those self-limiting beliefs and reframe it into a positive affirmation.

Identify 1 Statement that is Negative Self-talk

Create 3 Positive Affirmations

Repeat and Reinforce 2 Times a Day

How does this new perspective impact your sense of self and your approach to challenges?

_____
_____
_____
_____
_____
_____
_____
_____
_____
_____
_____
_____

NORMAN VINCENT PEALE

Norman Vincent Peale, a beacon of inspiration, transformed personal trials into triumph. As an influential author, minister, and speaker, he championed the power of faith and optimism. His journey from adversity to success is exemplified by his renowned work, "The Power of Positive Thinking." Peale's enduring legacy continues to guide individuals in conquering self-doubt and pursuing brighter futures, a testament to the strength found in unwavering faith and a positive mindset.

CHANGE YOUR THOUGHTS, CHANGE YOUR WORLD.
- NORMAN VINCENT PEALE

The lens through which you view life shapes your reality. Shift your thoughts, and watch
as the world around you transforms.

Journaling

MINDFULNESS IN ADVERSITY

Describe a situation where you felt overwhelmed. Practice mindfulness by fully immersing yourself in that memory and acknowledging your emotions without judgment.

_____
_____
_____
_____
_____
_____
_____
_____
_____
_____
_____
_____
_____

SHARON SALZBERG

A meditation pioneer and world-renowned teacher, Sharon Salzberg was among the first to bring meditation and mindfulness into mainstream American culture over 45 years ago. Sharon's dedication to mindfulness and loving-kindness meditation not only healed her own wounds but also illuminated a path for countless others seeking solace and inner strength. As a renowned author and meditation teacher, her journey is a testament to the healing potential of mindfulness in adversity. Sharon Salzberg's life story resonates as an inspirational beacon, guiding individuals toward self-compassion, resilience, and the realization of their full potential in the face of life's trials.

MINDFULNESS ISN'T ABOUT AVOIDING ADVERSITY; IT'S ABOUT FACING IT WITH A CLEAR MIND.

Mindfulness empowers you to confront challenges head-on, bringing clarity and calm to the chaos of adversity.

Journaling

Embracing Self-Compassion: List three things you appreciate about yourself. How can you show yourself the same compassion and understanding you'd offer a close friend facing a similar obstacle?

_____

_____

_____

_____

_____

_____

_____

_____

_____

_____

_____

_____

_____

_____

_____

CHRISTOPHER GERMER

Dr. Chris Germer is a clinical psychologist and co-creator of the Mindful Self Compassion program. Germer's journey is a beacon of hope for those navigating life's challenges. Chris' primary interest is self-compassion—the warmhearted attitude of mindfulness when we suffer, fail, or feel inadequate. He stumbled onto self-compassion in 2005 as a solution to his decades-long struggle with public speaking anxiety. His commitment to self-compassion and emotional healing has not only helped him overcome adversity but also inspired countless individuals to find solace and strength in self-acceptance.

SELF-COMPASSION

is simply giving the same kindness to ourselves that we would give to others.

Christopher Germer

Extend the same grace and understanding to yourself that you so effortlessly offer others; you deserve the kindness of your own heart.

Journaling

RECALL A MOMENT WHEN YOU HAD TO MAKE A TOUGH DECISION. HOW DID YOU BALANCE YOUR EMOTIONAL AND RATIONAL RESPONSES?

In this reflection, you're asked to remember a difficult decision-making situation where you had to balance your emotional and rational responses. Consider writing down the purely logical response to the situation and then the entirely emotional response. Afterward, contemplate what a balanced, middle-ground response would look like.

_____

_____

_____

_____

_____

_____

_____

_____

_____

_____

_____

DANIEL GOLMAN

As a psychologist and author, his path led to groundbreaking work on emotional intelligence and its transformative impact on personal and professional success. Goleman's pioneering research reshaped the way we view intelligence and its role in our lives. His unwavering commitment to emotional intelligence has not only helped him conquer his own hurdles but has also paved the way for countless individuals to embrace their emotional selves and achieve profound personal growth.

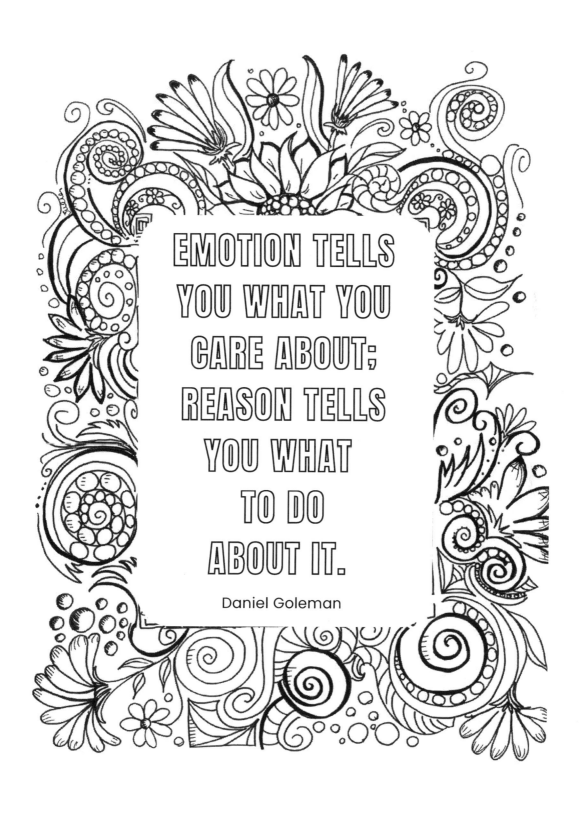

Your heart's feelings illuminate your values; let your mind guide you in transforming those feelings into purposeful actions.

Journaling

SETTING BOUNDARIES FOR GROWTH

Reflect on a relationship or situation that presents recurring obstacles. How can you establish and communicate healthy boundaries to facilitate personal growth and reduce friction?

_____
_____
_____
_____
_____
_____
_____
_____
_____
_____
_____
_____
_____
_____

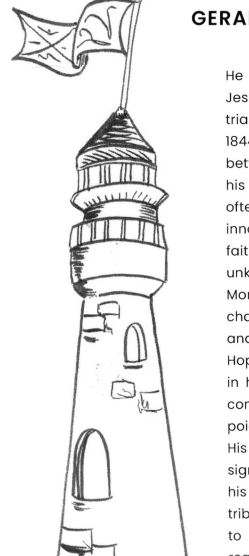

GERARD MANLEY HOPKINS

He was a renowned poet, and Jesuit priest, experienced profound trials throughout his life. Born in 1844, he struggled with the conflict between his religious vocation and his creative passions. His poetry, often characterized by its innovative style and themes of faith and nature, was largely unknown during his lifetime. Moreover, he faced personal challenges, including depression and a sense of isolation. Yet, Hopkins persevered, finding solace in his spiritual beliefs and a deep connection with nature, which he poignantly expressed in his poems. His posthumous recognition as a significant literary figure highlights his triumph over personal tribulations, as his works continue to inspire and resonate with readers worldwide.

"Your personal boundaries protect the inner core
of your identity and your right to choices."
Gerard Manley Hopkins

Create a Values-Based Decision Framework

Develop a systematic approach to incorporate values into your decision process:

- Identify the decision to be made
- List your relevant core values
- Evaluate how each option aligns with those values
- Assign a "values score" to each option
- Use the scores to inform your final choice
- This framework ensures you consciously consider values at each step.

Journaling

REFLECT ON YOUR EXPLORATION THUS FAR

Identify the topic or prompt that triggered the strongest resistance within you. With a gentle and curious spirit, delve into the inner workings of your internal system to understand why this particular prompt has caused distress. Could there be an aspect of you that is trying to protect you from memories, emotions or reactions? Approach this inquiry as if different aspects of you are sharing their perspectives on the resistance, fostering a compassionate dialogue within your inner landscape.

CARL JUNG

Carl Jung, a psychology pioneer, revolutionized our understanding of the human mind. Born in 1875, he tirelessly explored introvert-extrovert personalities, archetypes, and the unconscious's influence on our thoughts and behaviors. His groundbreaking work reshaped how we view ourselves and our inner worlds, leaving an enduring legacy in the field of psychology.

**THE PRIVILEGE OF A LIFETIME
IS TO BECOME WHO YOU TRULY ARE.
C.G. JUNG**

By defining your boundaries, you
affirm your right to self-respect
and clarity, creating a space
where your true self can thrive.

Consider the following practical steps to move to a more fulfilling and authentic life.

1. Self-Reflection
Take time regularly to reflect on your values, passions, and what makes you unique. Journaling can be an effective way to explore your thoughts and feelings.

2. Set Intentional Goals
Identify specific goals that align with your true self. Break these down into actionable steps you can take daily or weekly.

3. Practice Authenticity
Be honest about your feelings and opinions in conversations. Allow yourself to express who you are without fear of judgment.

4. Surround Yourself with Supportive People
Build relationships with individuals who encourage you to be your true self. Seek out communities that share your values and interests.

5. Embrace Vulnerability
Allow yourself to be vulnerable in safe spaces. Sharing your struggles and aspirations can deepen connections and foster authenticity.

6. Engage in Activities that Reflect Your True Self
Spend time doing things that resonate with your identity, whether it's pursuing hobbies, volunteering, or exploring new interests.

7. Limit Negative Influences
Identify and reduce exposure to people or environments that pressure you to conform or hide your true self.

8. Practice Mindfulness
Engage in mindfulness practices such as meditation or yoga to connect with your inner self and cultivate self-awareness.

9. Celebrate Your Uniqueness
Acknowledge and celebrate what makes you different. This could involve sharing accomplishments or simply appreciating your individuality.

10. Reflect on Progress
Regularly assess how far you've come in becoming who you truly are. Celebrate milestones and adjust goals as needed.

Journaling

EMBRACING THE MESSY MIDDLE OF CHANGE

Reflect on a pivotal transformation in your life. Recall the initial hurdles, the feeling of uncertainty, and the struggles you faced. As you journey through the challenging middle phase, consider the setbacks that altered your path. Then, reveal the beautiful outcomes and personal growth this change brought. Share the valuable lessons learned and how this transformation ultimately enriched your life. This reflection serves as a reminder that change, despite its difficulties, can lead to profound growth and beauty in the end.

_____

_____

_____

_____

_____

_____

_____

_____

_____

_____

ROBIN SHARMA

Robin Sharma is an internationally acclaimed author, motivational speaker, and leadership expert whose life journey is an inspiring testament to the power of personal transformation. Born in 1964, Sharma initially pursued a successful legal career before he embarked on a quest to uncover the secrets of personal and professional excellence. His relentless commitment to personal development and leadership led him to author numerous bestsellers, including "The Monk Who Sold His Ferrari." Through his books, speeches, and coaching, Sharma has touched the lives of millions, guiding them on a path toward greater purpose, productivity, and fulfillment.

"Change is hard at first, messy in the middle, and gorgeous at the end."
Robin Sharma

Consider the following practical steps as you transition and change:

1. Acknowledge the Difficulty
Recognize that change is challenging: Accept that initial resistance and discomfort are normal. Remind yourself that this phase is temporary and part of the process.

2. Set Realistic Expectations
Break down the change: Divide your goals into smaller, manageable steps. This makes the process less overwhelming and allows you to celebrate small victories along the way.

3. Embrace the Messiness
Be flexible: Understand that the middle phase may involve setbacks or confusion. Stay adaptable and open to adjusting your approach as needed.

4. Seek Support
Engage with others: Share your journey with friends, family, or colleagues. Their encouragement can provide motivation during tough times.

5. Reflect Regularly
Keep a journal: Document your thoughts and feelings throughout the change process. This can help you track progress and recognize patterns in your emotions.

Journaling

CELEBRATING UNIQUENESS:

WRITE ABOUT A TIME WHEN YOU FELT PROUD OF YOUR UNIQUENESS.

Recall a moment when you truly embraced your uniqueness and felt a sense of pride in being authentically yourself. Reflect on how this experience made you feel and the actions you took. Now, consider how you can bring more of that self-validation into your daily life. What steps can you take to honor your individuality regularly and express your true self in various aspects of your life?

_____

_____

_____

_____

_____

_____

_____

_____

_____

_____

HARVEY MACKAY

He's a renowned business author and motivational speaker, who has left an indelible mark on the world of entrepreneurship and personal development. Born in 1932, he overcame early struggles to become a prolific writer and speaker, known for his bestseller, "Swim with the Sharks Without Being Eaten Alive." Mackay's journey from humble beginnings to a successful businessman is an inspiring testament to the power of determination and business acumen. His insights on networking, leadership, and success have guided countless individuals and organizations, making him a source of inspiration and wisdom for those seeking to excel in their personal and professional lives.

Celebrate your individuality; it's the essence
of what makes you extraordinary.
Harvey Mackay

In a world of sameness, your individuality is a breath of fresh air. Celebrate it boldly, for it adds richness to the tapestry of life.

Journaling

Reflect on a specific area of your life where you'd like to introduce a positive change or new habit. Begin by acknowledging the challenge or resistance you might feel toward this change. Now, break down this transformation into the tiniest, most manageable "baby steps."

Writing down these initial, easy-to-achieve steps and the practical actions will allow you to make them a habit. Consider what motivates you to take these baby steps and how they can lead to more significant and lasting transformation. Embrace the power of incremental change as you embark on this journey of self-improvement.

_____
_____
_____
_____
_____
_____
_____
_____
_____
_____

WINSTON CHURCHILL

Winston Churchill, born in 1874, stands as one of the 20th century's iconic figures, celebrated for his unwavering leadership during World War II. His journey encompassed various political roles, including Prime Minister, Member of Parliament, and prolific writer. Churchill's resilience, unmatched oratory, and unyielding perseverance embody the essence of courage and tenacity. His legacy remains a testament to resolute leadership and an unwavering commitment to freedom and justice.

Striving for improvement invites growth; perfection is a journey of constant evolution, not a destination to be reached.

Closing Reflection

Each prompt has invited you to explore different facets of your inner world, from self-compassion and personal values to facing fears and embracing uniqueness. This introspective journey is ongoing, an ever-evolving exploration of your inner world. Each prompt has unveiled unique facets of your thoughts, emotions, and experiences, guiding your growth, building resilience, and enhancing your self-understanding.

As we conclude this empowering journey, it's essential to reflect on the transformative steps taken to nurture inner strength, empower confidence, triumph over challenges, celebrate uniqueness, and pursue dreams.

Unleashing Strength: Discover the wellspring of your inner strength and wisdom. Resilience, the foundation for inner peace, is harnessed through embracing this strength.

Empowering Confidence: Cultivate belief in your abilities, recognize your self-worth, and practice self-compassion and affirmation. Self-esteem becomes a cornerstone for tranquility.

Triumphing Over Challenges: Challenges are stepping stones for personal growth. Embracing this perspective hones resilience, cultivating fertile ground for inner peace.

Celebrating Uniqueness: Authentic self-expression and self-discovery stem from celebrating individuality, paving the path to pursue dreams and nurturing a sense of purpose.

MAY YOU FIND SOLACE, RESILIENCE, AND SELF-EMPOWERMENT ON YOUR ENDURING PATH OF SELF-DISCOVERY.

Julie True

Second American Edition 2024
True Hues Art LLC
Text and image copyright 2024 True Hues Art LLC
Images are hand drawn and personal property of Julie True
with the exception of geometric patterns.
The moral rights of the author have been asserted.
ALL RIGHTS RESERVED.

No part of this book may be reproduced, transmitted or stored in an information retrieval system in any form or by any means, graphic, electronic or mechanical, including photocopying, scanning, taping or recording, without prior written permission from the publisher.

TrueHuesArt.com | TrulyReflecting.com

Made in the USA
Columbia, SC
02 November 2024